A Robbie Reader

MONEY MATTERS: A KID'S GUIDE TO MONEY

# A KID'S GUIDE TO STOCK MARKET INVESTING

Tamra Orr

*Mitchell Lane*
PUBLISHERS

P.O. Box 196
Hockessin, Delaware 19707
Visit us on the web: www.mitchelllane.com
Comments? email us: mitchelllane@mitchelllane.com

*Mitchell Lane*
**PUBLISHERS**

# MONEY MATTERS
# A KID'S GUIDE TO MONEY

## Budgeting Tips for Kids
## Coins and Other Currency
## A Kid's Guide to Earning Money
## A Kid's Guide to Stock Market Investing
## Savings Tips for Kids

**ABOUT THE AUTHOR:** Tamra Orr is the author of more than 100 books for children of all ages, as well as several books and articles on money management and the stock market. She lives in the Pacific Northwest with her kids and husband and spends as much time reading as she can. Being an author is the best possible job she can imagine.

**PUBLISHER'S NOTE:** The facts on which the story in this book is based have been thoroughly researched. Documentation of such research can be found on page 46. While every possible effort has been made to ensure accuracy, the publisher will not assume liability for damages caused by inaccuracies in the data, and makes no warranty on the accuracy of the information contained herein.

**Library of Congress Cataloging-in-Publication Data**

Orr, Tamra.
  A kid's guide to stock market investing / by Tamra Orr.
     p. cm. —(Money matters—a kid's guide to money)
  Includes bibliographical references and index.
  ISBN 978-1-58415-642-0 (library bound)
  1. Stocks—Juvenile literature.
  2. Investments—Juvenile literature. I. Title.
  HG4661.O77 2009
  332.63'22—dc22
                                     2008002259

**Printing** 1 2 3 4 5 6 7 8 9

PLB

# Contents

Words in **bold** type can be found in the glossary.

# PART OWNERSHIP OF A BILLION BURGERS SOLD

The sounds of students talking, lockers slamming, and footsteps pounding filled the school hallway. Any minute, the morning bell would ring. In Mrs. Hudson's fifth-grade classroom, Sasha and Tim were already in their seats.

"What did you do over the weekend?" asked Tim. "Anything fun?"

"I went out for breakfast with my parents Saturday morning," said Sasha. "We went to McDonald's. They took me there because I love their pancakes and sausage."

"I'm glad you went there," said Tim, with a big grin.

"Why?" asked Sasha. "Do you like their pancakes too?"

Tim chuckled. "Well, no, I don't like pancakes at all, but that's not it," he said. "It's because I own part of McDonald's."

"You do not!" exclaimed Sasha.

"Yes, I do," replied Tim. "Well . . . maybe one ten-thousandth of it or so. My grandmother bought me a few stocks in McDonald's for my birthday. That makes me

part-owner of the restaurant. I watch the stock market reports every morning to see how it's doing."

Before Sasha could ask any more questions, Mrs. Hudson began taking attendance. When she was finished, Sasha raised her hand.

"Mrs. Hudson, what is the stock market?" she asked. "Can I actually own part of a big business like McDonald's?"

Mrs. Hudson paused for a moment, looking puzzled. "Where did that question come from?" she asked.

"I started it," replied Tim. He explained about the gift from his grandmother.

"Now I understand," said Mrs. Hudson. "Who else has heard of the stock market?"

About half the students raised their hands.

"Let's start at the beginning then. First, we need to learn a few simple terms." Mrs. Hudson walked over to the blackboard and began writing. She made two columns of words.

| | |
|---|---|
| stocks | stockholder |
| broker | shares |
| traders | stock report |
| dividend | bonds |
| risk | bull market |
| investment | bear market |

On a trading floor on Wall Street, traders watch stock market prices rise and fall on overhead monitors. Before New York City was a city, it was a Dutch colony. The Dutch built a wall in 1644 to protect against British attacks from the north. Years later, the wall was taken down, but the road next to it remained. That road became known as Wall Street—home of the country's financial center.

"Are any of these terms familiar to you?" she asked the class. Most of the kids shook their heads. Even Tim had not heard of some of the terms.

"First, let me answer Sasha's question. She asked me what the stock market is. To answer that, we first have to realize what a stock is. It is a piece of a business that other people can buy. They hope that by buying a piece of it, called a share, the business will succeed and they will end up making more money than they had before."

Mrs. Hudson could see that some of her students were still confused. "Look at it like this. Imagine that you make the world's best chocolate chip cookies. Everyone loves them, so you decide you want to start your own cookie making business. You know that to make enough cookies, though, you need a lot of supplies, like chips, sugar, flour, and butter— and maybe multiple ovens and pans. All those things cost money. If you don't have that money, how can you get it?"

"You could borrow it," said Jackie.

"You're right, you could," said Mrs. Hudson. "What else?"

"You could save up over time," said Theresa.

"True. Are there any other ideas?"

"You could ask your friends to help you," suggested Emilio.

"Exactly," said Mrs. Hudson. "And that is how stocks are started. You say to your friends, 'If you will give me some money, you can own part of my business.' They give you money for your supplies. Then, later, when your business takes off, you can pay them back their money plus a little extra—their share of your profit."

"What if the business doesn't succeed, though?" asked Sung.

"In that case, your friends might lose their money, and that is why buying stocks always carries a certain amount of risk," replied Mrs. Hudson. "Even with ones like McDonald's," she added.

"Here is what I'd like you to do next, " she continued. "Copy the list of words down in your notebooks. When you get home tonight, look each word up in the dictionary. Write out the definition you find, and then tomorrow, we will read them and see what everyone came up with." The students began pulling out their notebooks to write down the words.

"One more thing," added Mrs. Hudson. "I want you to get a copy of any newspaper from this week. Look up the stock market report, cut it out, and tape it into your notebook. It will look like some complex code to you, so don't worry about reading it yet. Bring it in and we will work to decode it together."

As everyone wrote down their homework assignments, Sasha leaned over to Tim. "Who knew that having breakfast at McDonald's could turn into a school lesson?" she asked.

"Pancakes always lead to trouble," Tim replied, grinning.

# BECOMING A STOCKHOLDER

Have you ever wanted to own a part of a company like Tim owns a little piece of McDonald's? If so, you are not alone. There are millions and millions of people who own stocks today. Some are rich and some are not. Some are retired and some are young. Some own a single stock in one company, and others have multiple shares in a handful of companies. Some schools and individuals practice investing by setting up a fake stock market. They follow the stock market reports to see what their money would have done had they actually invested.

If you're not one already, you can become a stockholder, too—although for most stocks, if you are still a **minor**, you will need your parents' permission and assistance. You can buy your own shares after you turn eighteen.

If you would like to invest in the stock market, do you know *why* you want to? It is important to realize your reasons.

Do you want to own stock in order to make money? You might make money; you might lose money.

Do you want to own stock just to learn about the stock market? Great—you will definitely learn about it.

Do you want to own stock as practice for the future? Wise idea.

Each one of these is a valid reason for investing in the stock market. Before you invest, you should know what you are doing. In the beginning, you might want to start with just one inexpensive stock. Since there are absolutely no guarantees that your stock will go up, you have to realize that you are risking your money when you invest. There are things you can do, however, to help lessen that risk. Let's take a look at a few of them.

> # Money Makers
>
> The Chinese philosopher Confucius once said, "If a little money does not go out, great money will not come in."

## Asking Questions

How can you begin to know what stock to buy when there are so many? One of the best ways is to ask yourself several important questions.

(1) What do you like to eat, wear, or use? What brand names are on each one of those things? Each of these products is known as a **commodity**. Commodities are food, metal, or other physical substances that can be

The *Wall Street Journal* is one of the most important U.S. newspapers for checking on financial news and the latest stock market reports.

bought or sold. Write down the names of your favorite commodities, and then look them up in the stock listings. 2) What do people really need? If there is a new toy out, it may be hot right now, but how long will that last? Try to choose stock in a company that has products or services that people need on a regular and continuing basis. For example, even if the economy is struggling, people will still need food and medication, as well as utilities such as water, gas, and electricity.

(3) How long has the company been around? If it is brand new, it might not be stable enough to trust. If it is a business that has a long track record, however, that is a strong indication that it has some reliability.

Tim knew that he liked to eat at McDonald's, even if he skipped their pancakes. He also knew that other people liked to eat there too—after all, they advertise "billions and billions served"! He was also aware that this was a company that had been around for many years.

## Doing Homework

Next, do your stock market homework. For the next month, look in the newspaper every day and track how your stock is doing. Write it down in a notebook. After you have done this for 30 days or so, look it over carefully. How well did the stock do? Did it stay fairly steady, or were there some major ups and downs? You want something that seems reliable, not prone to roller-coaster values.

What else can you do? You can call a **brokerage firm** and ask for information on the companies in which you are most interested in investing. You can even call or email the companies and request a copy of their **annual reports** so that you can see how they have been doing for the past year.

## Buying Stocks

Once you have made your decision, it is time to contact a stockbroker—a person whose job it is to sell and buy shares or stocks for other people. Make sure to have your parents along for all the paperwork—and to give their permission. You might even have to rely on them for some of the bucks if your allowance or savings don't cover the cost of the shares you are buying. Some companies will allow minors to buy

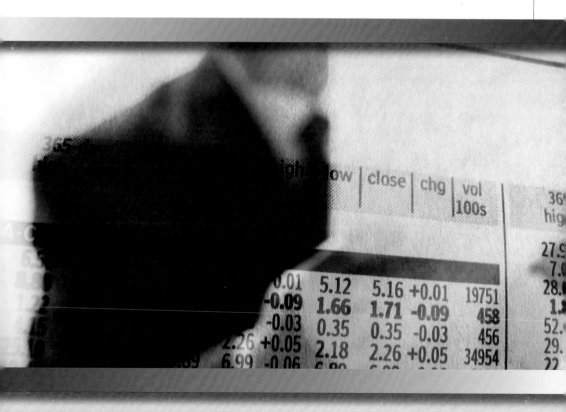

The value of stocks is printed in most major newspapers, but it can seem like a foreign language until you learn what each number means.

smaller amounts of stocks for less money, but you may have to have your stockbroker help you find out which ones. If you do not have the cash right now, you can still learn about the market. Pretend that you do have the money, and then follow the market to see what would have happened to your investment.

Whether you buy real or imaginary stock, sit back and see what happens. Keep checking those daily stock listings to see how well your share does. How long you keep it before deciding to sell depends on how it performs and what your goals are. If your company does poorly and loses money, you

You can find out how your stock is doing 24 hours a day, 7 days a week by going online.

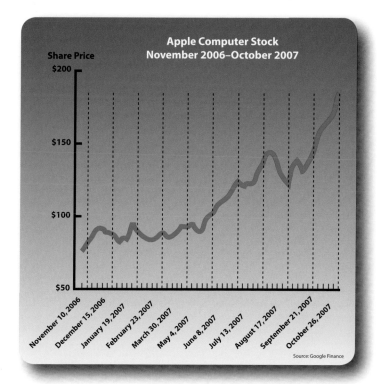

**Apple Computer Stock**
**November 2006–October 2007**

Share Price

$200

$150

$100

$50

November 10, 2006
December 15, 2006
January 19, 2007
February 23, 2007
March 30, 2007
May 4, 2007
June 8, 2007
July 13, 2007
August 17, 2007
September 21, 2007
October 26, 2007

Source: Google Finance

The longer you can track a stock's performance, the better you can figure out how reliable it is. Thirty days gives you a rough idea, but an entire year paints a more detailed, accurate picture.

might want to sell your share before its value is all gone. If you have time, however, you might want to let it ride and see if things turn around. If your share does well, you might want to sell it while it is riding high so that you can make a good profit, or what is technically called capital gain. If you are still not in a hurry, though, let it go and see if it just keeps going up. Investing is often a "wait and see" project.

Owning even a small piece of a company can be exciting. In many companies, owning a single share is enough to buy you voting rights. You might get the chance to vote on who sits on the board of the company. Board members make important decisions. If you own McDonald's stock, for example, your vote might eventually affect whether McDonald's adds another chicken sandwich or a new flavor of pie!

# Chapter

# LEARNING THE TERMS, CRACKING THE CODE

When you come home from school and your parents ask you how your day was, you might tell them every detail of your classes, friends, teachers, and homework, or you might think for a moment and then summarize it all into a couple of sentences. Summarizing the daily stock exchange action is what the Dow Jones does.

Dow Jones is a financial news publisher that researches the stock market. To figure the Dow Jones Industrial Average (DJIA), the agency looks at the closing prices of 30 specific stocks and then averages their performance. If the average shows that these stock values went up, DJIA reflects that the overall stock market value is going up. If the average shows a loss, however, the DJIA reflects the downturn.

Before you can understand how any industry works, you have to understand the technical terms, or **jargon**, it uses. Otherwise, you'll get lost quickly. To follow stock market investing, knowing the terms is extremely important.

Here are some common stock market terms:

Bear market: A period in which the stock market does poorly and the values are down.

Bond: A certificate of debt (saying, "We owe you") sold by businesses and governments to raise money.

Bull market: A period in which the stock market does well and the values are up.

Capital gain: The amount a stock rises in value between the time you buy it and the time you sell it.

Commission: The money paid to a stockbroker for doing his or her job of buying and selling stocks.

Commodity: A food, metal, or other material or product that investors buy or sell.

Crash: When a stock or stocks lose most of their value very quickly.

Dividend: A share of the profits from the business that is given to the stockholder. There are cash dividends and stock dividends.

Dow Jones Industrial Average: A number that shows the average closing prices of 30 industrial stocks, often referred to simply as "the Dow." Dow Jones also keeps track of other groups of businesses and provides their averages.

Exchange traded funds: Baskets of stocks put together and sold as one.

Investor: Someone who uses money to make money.

Penny stocks: Stocks not listed on a major stock exchange because they typically sell for $5 or less.

Risk: The likelihood of losing your money because a stock goes down in value instead of up.

Share: A part of a company that may be bought by someone as an investment.

Split: An increase in the number of shares in a corporation without changing the value of the total shares.

Stock: The money raised by a corporation through selling shares.

Stockbroker: A person who buys and sells shares of stock for other people.

Stockholder: A person who owns stock or has a limited amount of ownership rights in a company.

Stock market: A market in which shares of stock are bought and sold.

Stock report: A report that explains how a stock is performing overall.

Trader: Someone who buys and sells stocks or bonds in the financial markets.

## Cracking the Code

If you sit down with a newspaper like the *Wall Street Journal* or perhaps even your city's daily newspaper, take a look at the stock listings, usually found in the financial section. They are printed in tiny type, so you might need a magnifying glass to see it all clearly. They are also printed alphabetically according to their ticker symbols, so you will have to know the symbols to know where to find your stock listing.

At first glance, you may think each listing looks like some kind of foreign language that is made up of numbers. In a way that it is exactly what it is. It tells you a great deal of information, but you have to understand the code first before you can begin to **decipher** it. Here is an example of what one listing might look like:

| Stock | Ticker Symbol | Close | Volume | 52-Week High/Low | Dividend | EPS | P/E |
|-------|--------------|-------|--------|------------------|----------|-----|-----|
| McDonald's | MCD | 54.78 | 14,437,621 | $63.69/$42.50 | 0.38 | 1.93 | 27.84 |

| **Match the Numbers to the Definitions Below** | | | | | | | |
|---|---|---|---|---|---|---|---|
| 1 | 2 | 3 | 4 | 5 | 6 | 7 | 8 |

1. **Stock:** The basic name of the stock.

2. **Ticker symbol:** A one- to six-letter code used to identify the stock.

3. **Close:** The price paid per share at the end of a day of trade. If the company is doing well, this closing number will go up over time.

4. **Volume:** The number of shares that were bought and sold during one day of trading (more than 14 million!)

5. **52-week high/low:** The highest and lowest prices of the stock in the previous year.

6. **Dividend:** The portion of the profits to be paid to the stockholders.

7. **EPS:** Earnings per share—A company's profits over the previous year divided by the number of shares. The EPS will go up if the company is doing well.

8. **P/E:** Price-to-earnings—A **ratio** determined by dividing the current price of a share of stock by how much the company has earned per share over the previous year.

# Common U.S. Ticker Symbols, with Logos

**General Electric Company**
Symbol: GE

**Apple, Inc.**
Symbol: AAPL

**Coca-Cola Company**
Symbol: KO

**McDonald's Corporation**
Symbol: MCD

**Ford Motor Company**
Symbol: F

**Walt Disney Company**
Symbol: DIS

**Toys "R" Us**
Symbol: TOY

**The National Footbal League**
Symbol: NFL

**Wal-Mart Stores, Inc.**
Symbol: WMT

**Microsoft Corp.**
Symbol: MSFT

Now that you know the jargon and can understand the code, the stock market should make a lot more sense to you overall. You can now read about several stocks, pick the one that most interests you, and then follow it to see how it performs. Choosing what shares to buy takes thought and homework—but if you can speak the language, your work will be easier.

Thomas Edison made many improvements to the ticker tape machine, which kept track of stock prices and printed them out. His model was the most successful one of all. Today, stock market prices are recorded and displayed electronically.

## A Few Bonuses

Some companies make a special effort to make it fun for kids to invest in them.

- The William Wrigley Jr. Co. sends each stockholder a 100-stick box of gum at the end of the year.

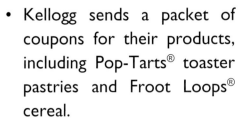

- Kellogg sends a packet of coupons for their products, including Pop-Tarts® toaster pastries and Froot Loops® cereal.
- 3M, for just a small fee, offers holiday gift boxes of products like tape and Post-it® sticky notes.

Epcot Center at Disney World in Florida. Some of the companies that allow kids to buy small shares of stock are Disney, General Motors, and McDonald's.

# THE WORLD OF STOCK EXCHANGES

**4**

The heart of buying and selling stocks can be found at the world's stock exchanges. They are loud places, with thousands of people constantly shouting "Buy!" and "Sell!" or yelling out prices as they rise and fall. Some people have said the action resembles a huge hive of angry bees or a verbal traffic jam. Stock exchanges are definitely hectic places, but they are exciting, too. They have been like this since 1817, when stock markets first opened.

## The New York Stock Exchange

There are three main stock exchanges in the United States. The largest and oldest one is the New York Stock Exchange (NYSE), located on Wall Street in Manhattan, New York's financial district.

The NYSE is run by a board of directors, and there are 1,366 membership seats. It was formed in 1792 by a group of 24 brokers who met underneath a buttonwood tree in what is now Battery Park. Originally called the Stock Exchange

The financial district in New York City was the site of a terrorist assault long before the attack on the World Trade Center on September 11, 2001. On September 16, 1920, at about noon, a horse-drawn carriage pulled up in front of the J. P. Morgan Building on Wall Street. A bomb exploded minutes later, killing 35 people and injuring hundreds more. The building still has marks on it from this decades-old attack.

Office, it did not adopt its new name until 1863. Members had to be voted in, and they had to pay for their seat. Only the most **elite** in society were included. In 1817, the cost of a seat was $25. In 1827, the price had quadrupled to $100. By 1848, it had quadruped again to $400. In 1888, the cost was up to $4,000, and in 2008, seats could be sold for as much as $1 million. By 2008, the most paid for any single seat was $2.65 million.

When the NYSE first opened, its members wore top hats and swallowtail coats to work each day. Women were not allowed through the front door. Today, most of the members wear dress shirts, slacks, and ties, and there are many female traders and members.

What happens inside is a little like watching a pond after a stone is thrown into it. The ripples just keep expanding outward.

First, since 1953, the morning bell rings at 9:30 A.M. Eastern Standard Time. Immediately, phones begin to ring constantly. Each call is an order from a company, stockholder or other concerned group to buy or sell a stock. The order is then transferred from the first broker to one of hundreds of booths on the trading floors. The people who take those orders are called floor brokers. They pick up the orders and take them down to trading posts, where specialists who represent certain groups of stocks wait. These workers yell out the highest bids to buy stocks or the lowest offers if they want to sell. They keep yelling these numbers until they meet in the middle and make a deal. Usually all eyes are on the lit board up on the wall, which constantly scrolls with the price of each stock and is updated every few minutes. The closing bell rings at 4:00 P.M. and everyone goes home. The stock markets stay closed on holidays and weekends.

Even as far back as 1880, the stock exchange was a bustling place. A man named William Worthington Fowler described brokers when he wrote, "They are all eyes and ears, scud and scamper, their fingers quivering like aspen leaves, their mouths pouring out a stream of bids and offers." He added

The London Stock Exchange in London, England, traces its history back to 1698. It began in a coffee house, and today it lists 2,600 companies, which represent 55 countries.

that they are able to send all their messages through "ten digits [their fingers] and with nods and winks."

## The American Stock Exchange

Another stock exchange is the American Stock Exchange, known as AMEX. It is the second largest and is also located in New York City. It began in 1849 with a group of brokers who wanted to be part of the NYSE but could not afford to buy a seat. Instead, they traded stocks and bonds much more informally outside on the streets, earning them the nickname of The New York Curb Agency. By 1921 they had grown so large and so loud that they were forced to move inside a building on Trinity Place—the same place it is located today. From 1929 to 1953, it was known as the New York Curb Exchange, or Curbstone Brokers, but then it changed its name to the American Stock Exchange. Today, AMEX is known for trading a type of stocks called exchange traded funds, which are baskets of stocks put together and sold as one.

## Money Makers

Looking fierce and powerful, the 7,000-pound bronze Charging Bull statue sits in New York City's financial district. It was created after the 1987 stock market crash by artist Arturo Di Modica. He said he built it as a symbol of the "strength and power of the American people."

## The NASDAQ

The third exchange is the NASDAQ, which stands for the National Association of Securities Dealers Automated Quotation. NASDAQ is the first and largest electronic stock market in the world. It started in 1971. Instead of being a big

The New York Stock Exchange bustles with traders manning computers on the floor. NASDAQ operates differently because people can log in remotely.

room with yelling people, it is an automated, computerized information system that provides price quotations to brokers and dealers. Because it is electronic, people can connect from anywhere. It is the fastest-growing company of them all.

In 1998, AMEX and NASDAQ merged to create the NASDAQ-AMEX Market Group, but they still operate as two separate companies. Along with these three main stock exchanges, there are smaller ones in large cities throughout the United States, including Chicago, Arizona, Kansas City, Minneapolis, Boston, and Philadelphia. A company is traded on only one market at a time.

## International Stock Exchanges

Of course, the United States is not the only country that has stock exchanges. There are stock exchanges around the world, including several in Africa, more than two dozen in Asia, 34 in Europe, 5 in the Middle East, 7 in Canada, 1 in Mexico, and 15 in South America.

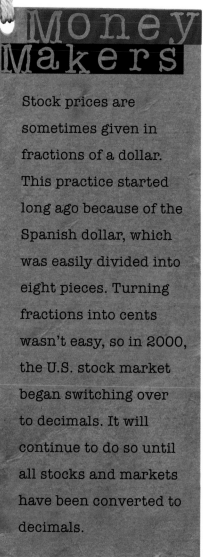

# Money Makers

Stock prices are sometimes given in fractions of a dollar. This practice started long ago because of the Spanish dollar, which was easily divided into eight pieces. Turning fractions into cents wasn't easy, so in 2000, the U.S. stock market began switching over to decimals. It will continue to do so until all stocks and markets have been converted to decimals.

# Chapter 5

# SURVIVING A CRASH

It does not happen often—thank goodness. In fact, it has happened only twice since 1792. Even so, when it happens, it causes panic, fear, and confusion. It is a financial disaster known as a stock market crash.

## The Stock Market Crash of 1929

The 1920s were a great time in U.S. history. World War I was over. Radios and automobiles were hot new inventions. The economy was climbing and climbing. It is no surprise that the decade was referred to as the Roaring Twenties. One thing that roared the loudest was the Dow Jones Industrial Average. It was soaring straight up, and investors responded by snapping up as many shares as possible. They were not remotely worried about risk because the economy was too strong to even consider anything bad happening. From 1921 to 1929, the stock market's value increased by more than seven times. What was worth 10 cents was now worth almost 70 cents! That was a huge growth. People became millionaires in

People flocked out to the street on Black Thursday, October, 24, 1929. Their faces reflect the fear, confusion and worry that day brought to so many families. It was the beginning of the Great Depression.

a matter of days. With wild abandon, people invested their life savings in the stock market. They **mortgaged** their homes in order to buy stocks.

The unthinkable happened in October 1929. For weeks, the stock market had been going up and down over and over. Some experts compared it to the tremors that often come before a huge earthquake. The government had raised the interest rate a few times to balance the stock market, and it went too far. Stock prices began to plummet. People

**Unemployment Rose**

**Housing Market Dropped**

# Stock Market Crash of 1929

**BROOKLYN DAILY EAGLE**

**WALL ST. IN PANIC AS STOCKS CRASH**

*Attempt Made to Kill Italy's Crown Prince*

**Supply and Demand**
**up          down**

**Interest Rates Rose**

Several factors brought about the 1929 stock market crash. A growing number of people were out of work (unemployment). The buying and selling of homes (housing market) had slowed down considerably. The government had raised the interest rates charged on bank loans (interest rates), and for many companies production was at an all-time high—but demand for their goods was slipping (the supply was greater than the demand). Each of these factors, and several others, contributed to the Stock Market Crash of 1929.

panicked. Stockholders wanted to cash in their shares. The stock market fell from 400 points to 145. More than $5 billion in stock value was lost in less than three days. By end of the crash, $16 billion was gone. Stocks became worthless once there was no money behind them to make them valuable.

The problems didn't stop there, however. The banks had taken money from their customers and invested it in the stock market too. Now they had no money to give to people when they came to claim it. Accounts were empty. More than 10,000 banks failed, and former millionaires became very depressed and worried.

The effects of the stock market crash of 1929 were widespread. The damage to the economy launched the Great Depression, a time of mass poverty. Workers lost their jobs. Families lost their homes. The Great Depression lasted until the mid-1930s, and the stock market did not regain its losses until 1955.

## The Stock Market Crash of 1987

Almost exactly 58 years later, the second stock market crash occurred. On October 19, 1987, the Dow Jones lost 22.6 percent of its value—equal to $500 billion. The stocks that just a few minutes before were high in value became worth very little, often less than what people had paid for them in the first place.

Both 1986 and 1987 had been good years for the stock market. People were investing heavily in another new technology: personal computers. Thousands of Internet companies, called dot-coms, were starting up. Because so many people believed the dot-coms would make millions, they invested in those, too. All that investing in only a few types of companies created what is called a bubble.

In October 1987, the bubble burst, and the stock market tumbled. As the news spread and investors heard of the crash, they flooded brokers' offices with phone calls, crying, "Sell! Sell! Sell!" It was too late. People lost millions in minutes. Stock exchanges shut down early for the day. Brokers began selling off people's entire portfolios, or groups of stocks, rather than just one stock at a time. This resulted in a huge sell-off that spun out of control. (Today, if brokers see a potential sell-off brewing, the trading stops until the market has a chance to cool off and become stable again.)

The government stepped in before a second Great Depression could begin. It closed all the U.S. banks for three days. When they reopened, there were strict limits on how much money a person could withdraw from his or her account. Within a few days, the stock market had rallied. Many people felt they had learned an important lesson about investing wisely. The government also

set up the **Federal Deposit Insurance Corporation**, or FDIC. The purpose of the FDIC is to guarantee that if a bank goes **bankrupt** or out of business, people who had accounts with that bank would not lose all their money. This helped people feel safer in investing again.

## Making Predictions

With crashes like the ones of 1929 and 1987, it is understandable that people want a reliable way to predict what the stock market will do. There truly is no such thing, although those who study economic history and follow the market very closely may be able to make more educated guesses than others. While many economists may use complicated calculations and fancy formulas to come up with their best predictions, other investors use some more unusual and even amusing methods to predict how the stock market will perform.

For example, ever since the first Super Bowl football game in 1967, some investors began to believe that if the National Football Conference team won the game, it would be a good year for stocks. On the other hand, if the team from the American Football Conference won, it would be a bad year for stocks. Does the Super Bowl have anything to do with stock market performance? No, but it is fun to compare them.

Another theory, the January Effect, has been shown to be right about 90 percent of the time. The theory says that if stock prices rise for the first week or even the entire month

In early 2008, people felt some of the same tremors in the stock market as were felt in 1929. The housing market slowed down, and people lost their homes as interest rates rose. Unemployment was on the rise, and gasoline prices were hitting record highs. U.S. lawmakers began looking for new ways to safeguard the economy.

of January, they will be up for the rest of the year. While hardly scientific, these theories do make stockholders smile.

Investing is far from a sure thing—you can lose your money. However, you can also break even or make a profit. At the same time, you can learn much more about how the economy works, how corporations are run, and how you can be a part of both!

# IT'S NEVER TOO EARLY

"So, did you have breakfast at McDonald's again this morning?" Tim asked as he and Sasha walked over to their desks.

"Not this time," Sasha said with a smile. "Mom just made me some toast and jam today."

"No wonder my stock dropped," Tim replied with a grin, and Sasha laughed.

"Okay, everyone, let's take a look at what all those financial terms mean," said Mrs. Hudson. The classroom was filled with the sounds of papers being pulled out of notebooks. For the next thirty minutes, the students went over the words and discussed what they meant in relation to the stock market.

"Now, let's move over to the computer lab," said Mrs. Hudson. "Today each one of you is going to become an investor."

"I didn't bring any money to school today," said Jackie.

"Don't I need my parents' permission first?" asked Emilio.

Mrs. Hudson chuckled. "Don't worry. I don't need any money from anyone. We are going to go online to a special web site that allows us to invest pretend money in a stock and then follow it over the next few weeks to see what happens to it. It will help each of you get a better idea of how the

Some sites that offer fantasy investing are How the Market Works (http://www.howthemarketworks.com/trading/index.php), Investopedia (http://simulator.investopedia.com/), National Stock Market Simulations (http://www.nationalsms.com/), and the Stock Market Game (http://www.smgww.org/).

Financial advisers can help answer your questions about stocks and give you professional advice on what to buy—or not buy.

market works—for the day when you might choose to invest some money in it. It's never too early to give it a try."

As the students made their way across the hall to the lab, Sasha whispered to Tim, "I'm going to invest my money in McDonald's. I am already missing those pancakes!"

## Books

Barbash, Fred. *The Stock Market*. Philadelphia: Chelsea House Publishers, 2002.

Bochner, Arthur, and Rose Bochner. *The New Totally Awesome Money Book for Kids*. New York: New Market Press, 2007.

Caes, Charles. *The Young Zillionaire's Guide to the Stock Market*. New York: Rosen Publishing Group, 2000.

Davidson, Avelyn. *The Bull and the Bear: How Stock Markets Work*. San Francisco: Children's Press, 2007.

Fuller, Donna Jo. *The Stock Market (How Economics Work)*. Minneapolis: Lerner Publishing Group, 2005.

Karlitz, Gail. *Growing Money: A Complete Investing Guide for Kids*. New York: Price Stern Sloan, 2001.

Lange, Brenda. *The Stock Market Crash of 1929: The End of Prosperity*. Philadelphia: Chelsea House Publications, 2007.

McGowan, Eileen, and Nancy Lagow Dumas. *Stock Market Smart*. Minneapolis: Millbrook Press, 2002.

Mayr, Diane. *The Everything Kids' Money Book: From Saving to Spending to Investing*. Cincinnati, Ohio: Adams Media Corp, 2002.

Zuravicky, Orli. *The Stock Market: Understanding and Applying Ratios, Decimals, Fractions and Percentages*. New York: Powermaths (Powerkids Press), 2005.

## Web Sites for Kids

Kids Konnect with the Stock Market
www.kidskonnect.com/content/view/296/27

Planet Orange Kids' Page
www.orangekids.com

Walley's Stock Ticker
www.prongo.com/stock/index.pl

Young Investor
www.younginvestor.com

## Works Consulted

Kelly, Jason. *The Neatest Little Guide to Stock Market Investing*. Revised edition. New York: Plume, 2007.

Lynch, Peter. *One Up on Wall Street: How To Use What You Already Know to Make Money in the Market*. New York: Simon and Schuster, 2000.

Mahar, Maggie. *Bull!: A History of the Boom, 1982–1999: What Drove the Breakneck Market—and What Every Investor Needs to Know About Financial Cycles*. New York: Collins, 2003.

Mladjenovic, Paul. *Stock Investing For Dummies*. Second edition. New York: Wiley Publishing, 2006.

Sobel, Robert. *The Big Board: A History of the New York Stock Market*. Santa Ana, California: Beard Books, 2000.

## On the Internet

A to Z Investments www.atozinvestments.com

CNN's Money Page www.money.com

Eyewitness to History: The Wall Street Crash, 1929
http://www.eyewitnesstohistory.com/crash.htm

Stock Market Crash! Net www.stock-market-crash.net

The National Association of Investment Clubs
http://www.better-investing.org/Public/default?

# Glossary

**For terms related directly to stock market investing, see pages 20–21. Other words that may be unfamiliar to you are defined below.**

**annual report**—A record of a company's profit and loss over the previous year; it also includes any major operating changes in the company.

**bankrupt**—A person or company that owes more money than it earns and cannot possibly pay the debts already owed.

**brokerage firm**—A company that employs stockbrokers.

**decipher** (dee-SY-fur)—To decode or figure out.

**elite** (ee-LEET)—The highest section, such as the highest social class.

**Federal Deposit Insurance Corporation**—A government insurance company that guarantees that if a bank goes bankrupt or out of business, people who had accounts with that bank would not lose all their money.

**jargon**—The language, with its specific terms, used by a particular industry.

**minor** (MY-nur)—A person who is under the legal age for certain things; in most states, a minor is anyone under 18 years old for voting or opening a bank account; under 21 years old for participating in other adult activities.

**mortgaged** (MOR-gidjd)—Took out a bank loan against the value of something, such as a house.

**ratio** (RAY-shee-oh)—A number that shows how two values are related, such as the price of gas per gallon, or the price of a share related to the yearly profit of a company.